In the Mind of the Anxious Traveler

In the Mind of the Anxious Traveler

Poems by

John Johnson

Cover design by Shay Culligan
Cover image by Caroline Selfors

ISBN: 978-1-63980-192-3

Kelsay Books
502 South 1040 East, A-119
American Fork, Utah 84003
Kelsaybooks.com

Acknowledgments

I wish to thank Jen Burton, Anne Mitchell, Judy Gamble, Amie Whitmore, and all the members of my weekly writing circle who have enhanced my writing and whose insights greatly helped me improve the quality of this manuscript. An extra special thank you to my writing instructor and friend Susan Vespoli, who always inspires me to write and pursue my poetry with passion and care. And to the many people behind these poems—you may or may not know who you are, but I thank you for sharing these moments with me.

The following poems in this collection have been previously published in an earlier format by these outlets:

Burrow E-Journal: "Hamster Home Office"

Instant Noodles: "Therapy in Sedona, Arizona"

Poetic Sun: "Espresso Love"

Contents

Part I: Home Sick

The Buffalo Holy Trinity

At Saint Benedicts, Hosannas are not sung
       at 7:15 mass.
Without music, our family vacates the hardwood
       pews more quickly
having satisfied holy obligations
       and spiritual needs.
We race up Main Street to beat out the other
       Christian pancake eaters.
Two Apostles cut us off; we are third in line
       for the non-smoking section.

Sprawled across the breakfast table,
       The Buffalo News forecasts snow squalls.
Bottomless coffee cups and forty-niner
       flapjacks for the adults,
Dutch babies with powdered sugar
       and fresh strawberries for the children.
Caffeine and maple syrup will fuel us
       to the last destination.

The clock has not struck ten
       and the line is forming outside Child World.
As the door opens, we each take our own
       different routes to Aisle Four.
Divine intervention—
       the rare figure missing from my collection.
Mom—the fastest—grabs the only pristine
       Bobby "The Brain" Heenan doll.

The Buffalo Holy Trinity is complete:
       church, pancakes, toy wrestling men.

A Brown Trunk and a Black Sharpie

Canteens, socks, mess kits and underwear are
          strewn across the dining room,
A brown trunk will hold all my worldly possessions
          for the next week.
No item is packed 'til Mom uses
          her black sharpie to write my name.
We shuttle back and forth to J.C. Penny's
          to get what we still need.

She makes me traipse around in my hiking boots
          so I won't get blisters.
If it is unseasonably cold,
          a purple goose down sleeping bag.
If the cot in my tent is lumpy,
          an inflatable air mattress.
If someone steals my swimsuit,
          I will be skinny-dipping.
She marks it.

If it rains every day, a green poncho—
          extra-large—to keep me dry.
So I can practice my square knots
          and taut-line-hitches—smelly hemp rope.
In case I lose my sense of direction,
          a compass and fold-up map.
We even test the combination lock—
          twenty-four, eleven, double three.

My first-time leaving home,
          Mom obeys the Scout motto—Be Prepared!
"TOOTHPASTE!" she exclaims as we close the trunk.
          She marks it with the sharpie.

West End 2

Cram swimsuit clad kids in the brown Charger,
        but leave the beach balls behind.
The trunk is full with spackle buckets
        and putty knives and small shovels,
In our flip flops, we stop
        at the hardware store to buy a new roller.
"Wallpaper project?"
        the checkout asks.
"Going to the beach." Dad replies.

West End 2 has no pesky swimmers,
        only miles of raw materials.
Today our family will declare
        this beach is a construction zone.
We wear sunscreen like hard hats,
        while forewoman Mom directs our work.
The hot sun hardens the design,
        far away from the destructive waves.

Each wet sand granule shapes
        a perfectly proportioned pyramid.
Sandstone bricks surround
        a multilayered oblong doorway on the front wall,
Hieroglyphic symbols embossed with care
        translate loosely to "Beware!"
A mural of terracotta warriors
        carry sand thistle spears.

As the sun sets, pack up Charger.
        The construction site is closed.
The pyramid is left for the seagulls
        as it slowly blows away.

Greyhound Love

A blind busker screeches his violin
        into the bitter cold air,
Exhaust fumes turn snowflakes dirty brown
        before they hit the frozen ground,
In my goose down jacket, this lovestruck kid
        searches for the bus station.
A woman in a torn trench coat claims to be
        Gloria Vanderbilt.

Three cops walk past me with a look that suggests
        "You don't belong here, kid."
But our love has no bounds, finally having
        found my destination,
The rotating board in the Greyhound Bus station
        clicks as I follow her journey from
Binghamton to Ithaca to Geneva and soon to Rochester.

Underneath my jacket and grasped
        by leather gloves are
some dime-store roses. Anticipation builds
        as the large bus pulls up—
I make eye contact with her in the front seat,
        but the driver disrupts our hallmark moment
as the giant bus wheel almost squashes my foot.

But then she is in my arms—her red turtleneck
        and black gloves—
we kiss. The heat in a lusty dorm room
        will warm us when we get to campus.

Hamster Home Office

From my home office,
I stare down at Chewy in his cage.
He mimics everything I do . . .
I am both a role model and a target of his mockery.
I imagine his squeaky hamster voice counting to eight,
As my eyes gaze at each indistinguishable corner of my office.
I take a quick swig from my half-filled coffee mug,
He immediately slurps from the metal straw on his water bottle.
I have to log on to yet another zoom meeting.
He jumps on his hamster wheel,
mentally checking out as his little legs run.
I fight with the jammed window to get some fresh air,
He bangs on his cage door trying to reach the latch.
My floor is covered with file folders and papers
I am too lazy to pick up,
It reminds me of the wood chips that need
to be cleaned out of his cage.
I open the cage, and he darts away as fast as possible,
a hostage no more.
I know the feeling . . . maybe I should go outside.
But then he stops . . . fear getting the better of him.
I should probably go back to my office
where I have been for a year.
I sit back down and realize I never bought a hamster.
He stares at me and squeaks back—
　　　　"I do exist."

Visiting with Mr. Lincoln

The same orange and maroon Nike Pegasus
       sneakers on my tired feet.
The same first song on the Spotify playlist:
       Rage Against the Machine.
The same sequence of buttons start
       the timer on my Garmin six watch.

Taut legs pounding on the pavement
       down 19th Street, 1.34 miles.
I stop and make eye contact
       with Mr. Lincoln from the bottom of 87 stairs.
He just stares back, as if to ask
       "Why are you worrying today?"

I tip my sweat-stained Nationals cap,
       and trek back 1.34 miles.
Taut legs wobble with each strike
       of the pavement up 19th Street.
The reverse sequence of buttons stops
       the timer on my Garmin six watch.

The last song on the Spotify playlist:
       For Whom the Bell Tolls.
The waxy earbuds and damp
       Nationals Cap goes back in the gym bag.
I untie the orange and maroon Nike Pegasus sneakers.

Even though Mr. Lincoln never gives me the answers
       I seek from him, I will do it again tomorrow.

Espresso Love

In the corner, a sleepy-eyed scribe silently sips java.
Under his feet, a concrete canvas
splattered with spilt coffee and croissant crumbs.
A triumvirate of trees canopies
visitors from the morning sun.
The pastel pinks of preppy polos
complement the red wildflowers.
Grannies bloom in floral sun dresses,
mingling with nosy neighbors and Harvard professors.
While Dad attends to a panting dog
slurping water from a plastic cup,
his kids in pajamas eat
chocolate chip cookies for breakfast.
In the corner, a sleepy-eyed scribe takes a second sip.

The Double Decker Starbucks Near My House

Two floors—double the chance to feed my addiction to coffee.
Without you in the morning, I have severe problems!
A rash of thoughts break out as the voices in my head chit-chat,
only receding when I smell that bitter aroma
and take that first black sip.
I find others attracted to caffeine, milk, and sugar,
as I am not the only one who comes
to the double decker Starbucks to be stirred.

Martinis are not the only drink shaken not stirred.
Each morning the young man in a lab coat picked up his coffee.
Deliberately measuring in equal proportions his cream and sugar,
lost in thought contemplating chemistry problems.
Shaking his drink precisely ten times before he takes a sip.
The same routine every day, nary a word or time to chit-chat.

Bored by her banal chit-chat,
he hardly feels stirred.
Distracting himself by taking a sip,
a blind date might have seemed less threatening over coffee.
But all she does is talk about herself and her problems
Bitter like black coffee, not sweet like sugar.

The mother and her daughter argue:
"I don't need three packets of sugar."
Details of hemorrhoids and varicose veins are today's chit-chat
Why do people want to share gory details of their health problems?
No matter how old I am, talking
to her means the inner child is stirred
The caffeine fuels the flood of
inconvenient memories as we drink our coffee
A stronger drink needed to wash away childhood trauma with a sip.

Quietly in the corner she takes a sip,
watching as the neighborhood moms
fight over the last pink fake sugar.
They each wear the same bright white
tennis outfits and drink the same size coffee.
The complete lack of awareness
of the snobbery in their chit-chat.
Each one-ups the other,
escalating the extent to which they are stirred.
It is amazing what you can overhear when others air their
problems.

A start to this day portends many other problems.
Before he even takes the first sip,
head down on the phone, unable to be stirred.
His large torso collides with her petite frame next to the sugar.
Curse words are their chit-chat
when white dress shirt and silk tie meet black coffee!

Not all patrons' problems are solved with cream and sugar,
Trouble brews at the shop if they simultaneously sip and chit-chat,
But what observations are stirred up over an innocent cup of
coffee.

I Didn't Understand

Anticipation of the five a.m. alarm is worse
        than its shrill chirp,
The stress heightened by an impatient limo driver
        ringing my phone.
I check hand scratched lists so not to forget
        my CPAP mask and phone chargers.

Travel is more traumatic
        than puberty,
surging stress hormones leading
        to endless ruminations
about whether to check my bag and how early I arrive
        and should I fly with an empty stomach?
Security lines don't quell my pounding
        heart nor dry my clammy hands.

But my friend
        was different.
Not a week went by where he didn't declare
        he would be on the road again.
It didn't matter where he was going, and often
        it wasn't clear why a phone call wouldn't do.
But Starwood points were his badge of courage,
        and he never unpacked his travel bag—
the lines between home and hotel
        completely blurred.

The less he traveled, the more unhappy he was.
The more I traveled, the more unhappy I was.
I didn't understand—until he told me his secret.
I felt foolish.

Soccer Dad

I can't feel my face as the wind picks up,
and the metal bleachers adhere to my butt cheeks.
My stomach growling and a glance at my watch,
A reminder that 40-minute halves are an eternity.
The looming end of the game—and the season—
conjures waves of memories.

His talents are cerebral—
Unexpected stutter steps, creative dribbles, trash talking.
An angry five-year-old lecturing his pint size teammate
who with reckless abandon scored in the wrong net.
A combative twelve-year-old ready to throttle
a yellow card toting official.
Yawning and shivering, I snap back to now.
With goals in short supply, there is not enough time.
A sixteen-year-old man pushing beyond his limits
as he throws up on the sidelines.

Yawning and shivering, I race to his side.
"Well, at least I know I gave it all I had,"
he says with a wry smirk.
I put my arm around him and touch his
cold, sweaty shoulders.
"I am proud of you."
I am glad I am home for this moment.

Part II: On the Road

First Class Lounge

I wander an infinite terminal like
     a traveling zombie,
The other faceless travelers scurry
     in every direction.
The golden ticket to a layover oasis:
     my paper boarding pass.
Pristine white walls greet me, as four hanging clocks
     spanning four time zones—
London, Tokyo, Addis Abba, New York.
     Floor to ceiling windows peer
at jumbo jet tails emblazoned
     with "Air Lingus" and "Iceland Air."
The baggage carts and gas trucks are dwarfed
     as they shuttle between aircraft.
The buffet offers little bowls of mixed nuts
     and spicy orange puffs
and miniature boxes of Raisin Bran
     and Yoplait yogurts on ice.
Every beverage is labeled: HOT WATER,
     DECAF, FRENCH ROAST, WHOLE MILK.
And a bartender offers me a drink
     even though it is 10 AM here.
I am summoned over the garbled loudspeaker . . .
     your flight is now boarding.
Only 14 more hours of white knuckle flying
     till I touchdown at Dulles.
I grab a Poland Spring and pop
     an Ambien as I head to the gate.

Butt Cheeks in Tokyo

Two jetlagged tourists observe a spectacle
      they don't quite understand,
Juxtapose scantily clad, plus-sized warriors
      with butt cheeks exposed,

Next to silk-adorned, fan-waving gyojis
      enforcing the ancient rules.
Ringside Shimpans directionally seated
      to the East, West, and North.
Purification and preparation
      soberly executed.

The sacred rope-edged mud circle refreshed
      with a steel watering can,
Ceremonial salt cleanses evil spirits
      to erase the past,
Elaborate acrobatic rituals performed
      before the battle.

Large men raise their legs in the air,
      looking like dancers in a ballet.
Slapping their girth creates
      a guttural echo foreshadowing
the fleshy demolition derby
      of rubber skin not twisted metal.

With a bow and wave, the niceties conclude
      and the battle begins.
A fast side-step and push and the giant
      tumbles headfirst to the floor.
The loud silence of the hall
      only disturbed by two men cheering.

Therapy in Sedona, Arizona

angry rocks:
baby cheek red/ boiled lobster pink/ burnt maple syrup

mother nature's mirror:
snapping scorpions/ iguana imposters /codependent chameleons

talk therapy:
rattler rat-tat-tat / coyote cacophony / gila monster hizzles

core wounds:
mating praying mantis / black widow bite / voracious vultures

treatment:
smashing rocks.

South Beach Triathlon

Which is more jarring: the cold morning air
        or the skin-tight neon tri suit,
exposing flabby arms, nipples, and private parts?
        Loitering on the beach
I stand next to muscle ripped competitors
        with swim capped bullet heads
Waiting for the gun shot to send us
        headfirst into the Atlantic.

Barreling directly into the waves,
        jostling my stroke and my breath
Mouth full of water, and a foot to the face.
        Where is the orange buoy?
Zigzag to the beach, a maze of bikes
        all look the same to tired eyes.
Towel off, wet socks stick to too wet legs,
        sneakers, sunblock, helmet, go.

Pedal. Only 20 miles on closed roads . . .
        I thought it was a short flat course—it wasn't.
Exhaustion turns empty giant cruise ships
        into cheering spectators,
Gettin' jiggy apparition of Will Smith
        singing "Welcome to Miami!"
My legs keep spinning as a transition
        to the final four-mile run.

My heart and the South Florida sun are pounding.
        Run. Walk. Run. Walk. Walk.
Am I done? My way-too-buff trainer cheers
        as I cross the finish line.

Road Trip on I-10 Between New Orleans and Houston

Our rented Chevy Suburban reverberates like a jackhammer—
as the cement highway rocks the well-worn tires.
And then the road leads us to the edge of Lake Pontchartrain—
as if we are riding the luge at Splash World.
And then we see the fingerprints of Laura—
sharply splintered leafless trees and downed power lines,
And then we pass a billboard—
imploring us to call personal injury lawyer Morris Bart.
And then we mourn an alligator—
suffering from rigor mortis on the shoulder.
And then the SUV in front of us proclaims—
"Covid-19 is fraud" in chalk window paint,
And then we pass another billboard—
imploring us to call personal injury lawyer Morris Bart.
And then the passenger seat fails to recline—
evidenced by the dirty footprints on the dashboard,
And then twin flames reach to the heavens—
burning smokestacks emitting unknown chemicals,
And then a rapid swerve—
to avoid a truck tire in the middle of the left lane,
And then we pass another billboard—
imploring us to call personal injury lawyer Morris Bart,
And then an invitation—
to hold a baby alligator at Exit 64,
And then a low flying crop duster—
covers the roof of our SUV in some unknown substance,
And then the fuel light goes on—
we exit the highway to refill at the Cheep Cheep gas station,
And then we pass another billboard—
imploring us to call personal injury lawyer Morris Bart.

The Road to Gay's Seafood

Left turn at the rusted sign,
bouncing down an uneven tree-lined path.
Crab-red painted placards point
toward a wooden storm-battered shanty.
The dock like outstretched arms
welcoming returning boats back from the bay.
Galosh wearing fishing wizards work magic,
no eye of newt needed.

Boiling in a giant steel cauldron,
two dozen live crabs are submerged
facing a steamy final fate,
doused in more than a pinch of Old Bay.
The only one rule of picking crabs:
Prepare to get very messy.
He wields a wooden mallet
and rounded knife with reckless precision.

Although I am lost,
he exudes confidence in me as always.
The first crack of the shell reveals
another cavern to excavate.
Digging and digging, like forty-niners,
our gold nuggets are lump crab.
The remnants of our mess everywhere—
bowls filled with hollow shells and juice,

We watch the sunset from the back porch
and toast each other with Merlot.
The joy not measured by harvested fish
but by time with my brother.

Car Crash

The blind spot in the mirror
left him exposed.
He drove too fast,
always onto the next thing.
He was reckless behind the wheel,
lacking the compunction most of us have.
Only focused on the next destination,
as long as someone filled the seat.
Or if he was the passenger,
his head buried in his phone the whole time.
Things finally spiraled out of control,
as he selfishly drove the car into a ditch.
He walked away before the flames
from the crash were extinguished.
The only question left unanswered—
whether he realized I was hurt at all?

Hotel Kleptomaniac

Three lime-seasoned soap bars wrapped in olive tissue
      —the gateway drug,
Moisturized hands swipe lotion imbued
      with fake pine and yling-yling.
Foil packets of cheap coffee taste much better
      in waxy paper cups.
Stirring a religious awakening,
      he takes the Gideon Bible.

"Thou Shalt Not Steal" does not apply
      to his free samples.
For this frequent traveler, free breakfast
      and a free drink at the bar.
Rubbery buffet eggs can't be swiped,
      but tiny jars of jelly can.
The fourteenth consecutive week on the road
      stealing time from home life.

Sun sets in whatever random city
      as he plops down at the bar.
He orders the most expensive scotch on the rocks,
      it's free after all.
A redheaded lady approaches,
      sipping an apple martini.
She rubs against his moisturized hands,
      sliding him her room key freely.

He responds emptying his pockets,
      offering her ketchup and butter.
"Thou Shalt Not Commit Adultery,"
      a commandment he will not break.

Escape to the Hotel Gym

Even from the 19th floor, the cacophony of
        horns and sirens echo,
New York City refuses to go to sleep,
        and rudely keeps me up.
A single bed occupies every inch
        of the miniscule room,
and a tiny plasma TV fills the rest with light
        from a rerun of Friends.

Frustrated and groggy, I leave the one-windowed closet
        labeled "Room 1920"
and use my key card for entry to the closet
        labeled "Hotel Gym."
The scent of antiseptic wipes like smelling salts,
        wide awake now.
On the far wall, another tiny plasma TV plays
        the same Friends rerun.

There is only one treadmill that sticks
        on every third step as I run,
and my legs crammed to my chest as I pedal
        a bike with a stuck seat.
I trip over ten and twenty pound barbells strewn
        like undergarments.
Alternating push-ups and sit-ups and bicep curls
        work up a sweat.

Then I find refuge on a large, puffy, dirty,
        blue exercise mat—
laying on my back stretching,
        my eyes get heavy
        and I drift to sleep.

My Favorite Company Christmas Party

Not at the Ritz Carlton with bacon wrapped scallops
     and gin martinis,
Not dressed in my Sunday best with a freshly purchased
     Santa Claus tie,
Not at the Watergate with tours of Nixon's bungling burglars
     spy room,
Not with a deejay who predictably played Gangnam style
     every year,
No River Cruise navigating icy waters
     like the Titanic,
No buffet with carved roast beef with horseradish
     and mushroom gravy,
No red and green macarons or cream dolloped
     pecan pie finger tarts,
No after party corralling of intoxicated
     coworkers,
No hotel, but a fire pit in a backyard,
     bundled in sweatshirts and hats.
Three chairs sit in a socially distant
     equilateral triangle,
Minimizing the pandemic risk that thrust us
     into loneliness.
Laughter replacing music, Christmas cookies
     replacing macarons,
M&Ms are our hors d'oeuvres, hot black coffee
     warms us better than bourbon,
The gift of friendship heightened by stepping out from
     behind a ZOOM screen.

Why I Fly

Because I always wondered what was above the clouds
and my parents moved me far away
from my girlfriend the day after graduation.
Because my girlfriend and I got married in Buffalo,
but we didn't want to honeymoon in Niagara Falls,
and because the Eiffel Tower
is much more impressive in person than on a postcard.
Because everyone I love is not within driving distance,
and my best college friend ended up
living exactly 2,292 miles from my home.
Because the bag of honey roasted peanuts on the plane
always leaves you wanting more,
and because I wrote a book on statistics
that explains it is safer to fly than drive a car.
Because I always wondered what was above clouds,
and everyone I love is not within driving distance.
Because my kids wanted to meet Mickey Mouse
and a client in Budapest needed me to visit a bus factory
and a guys' weekend is much better in Vegas than at a local bar.
Because everyone I love is still not within driving distance,
and I never would have known how big the world is
if I never learned to fly.

About the Author

John Johnson is a poet who loves language but also data and numbers. He resides in Northern Virginia where in addition to running his consulting firm as a professional econometrician, he loves pizza and professional wrestling and regularly writes with his wild writing circle. John's poetry tends to focus on humorous aspects of his geeky childhood and his journey as it relates to entrepreneurship, family, friendship, and failed athletic endeavors. His website is poemsovercoffee.com. He is the author of *Chalk Dust Memories* from Plan B Press.